I0091081

What Friends SHOULD Do

What Friends SHOULD Do

Discover If Your Friends Are Really Your Friends

Fred Mogura

SLP

Simple Logic Publications

WHAT FRIENDS SHOULD DO

Copyright © 2018 Thomas R. Morris All rights reserved. No part of this book may be reproduced or transmitted by any means or in any form without the prior written consent from the author or publisher. This includes photocopying, scanning, storing in or transmitting by any computer-based device or system.

Disclaimer: This book has been created for the purpose of entertainment. The author and publisher make no representations or warranties of any kind with respect to this book or its contents. The author and publisher and any of its employees disclaim any and all liability for any damages arising out of or in connection with this book. This includes, but is not limited to, distress, offense or insult. Any use of this book or its content is at the reader's own risk.

ISBN 978-0-9872677-8-8 (Trade Paperback)

For information, please contact the publisher at:
information@simplelogicpublications.com

Please note that we do not accept unsolicited manuscripts.

Illustrations under license from istockphoto.com,

Printed in Australia • United Kingdom
• United States of America •

020222

Table of Contents

PART 3

Support Each Other

PART 4

The Right Thing

PART 5

Walk the Walk

PART 6

Respect Each Other

PART 7

Consider One Another

PART 8
Be a True Friend

Introduction

Maybe your mom and dad are your friends. That would be great. Maybe your brothers and sisters are your friends. That too would be nice. Surely your partner is a friend and the people you mess around with are friends. Then there are people who you went to school with or now work with who you call a friend. And maybe you think all of those "friends" on Facebook are friends. But are these people *really* your friends? Are you theirs?

You need to ask yourself – Do the people you think are *friends* do or fail to do things that you expect a friend to not do or to do? Does it seem like they have forgotten what it means to be a *friend*? Or could it be that they don't have a clue what it takes to be a friend?

Do some of your *friends* get irritated, even upset with you for things you do or don't do? Could it be that *you* have forgotten or don't *really know* what it means or takes to be a friend?

If so, this book is for them, and you.

This book takes a fun but serious look at what *real friends* do. It looks at the things that make someone a real friend. Things like: accepting us for who we really are, and telling us if we have a big honking zit on our face – when we do.

So, what does it really mean to be a "friend"? What does it really take to be a *real* "friend"?

If we look in a dictionary or google the word *friend*, we may find something such as, a person with whom one has a bond of mutual affection. We may find that it means someone who shares common interests with us and gets pleasure out of doing those things together with us.

We may find that a *friend* is someone who tells us how it is, the good and the bad – someone who tells us things that we might not want to hear about ourselves. We may also find that a *friend* is someone who is genuinely interested in and concerned about what we say and do. And we might find that a friend is someone who encourages us to achieve our goals and dreams, to become who we wish to be and to do what we desire to do in and with our life.

So with that, let's get started, let's find out what friends *should* do – things that makes someone a real friend.

Please note: In this book, the word *partner* refers to one's boyfriend, girlfriend, legal, common-law or self-proclaimed wife or husband, whether heterosexual or LGBTQ.

PART 1

Tell How It Really Is

True friends stab you in the front.

(Oscar Wilde 1854 – 1900)

1

Friends tell their friends if they have a big honking zit on their face.

The same applies to boogers hanging out of our nose, bad breath, body odor and things stuck in between our teeth or hanging out of our mouth.

Real friends don't hold back the facts for a few laughs at the expense of a friend. A real friend wouldn't let their friend walk around all day or night wondering why people are looking at or pointing at them – unaware of any freaky or smelly stuff that is sticking out of or coming from their body. A real friend will tell us immediately when they notice something that needs our attention (things like zits, boogers, or B.O.).

A friend who sends us an email after an evening out to let us know that for the past 5 hours we had a monster zit, a green thing hanging out of our nose, or that we reeked isn't a real friend.

2

Friends tell their friends that their driving skills suck, when in fact they do.

Rather than remaining silent and holding on for dear life when riding in a car driven by a friend whose driving sucks, a *real friend* will tell that friend that it's time that they learn how to drive. This could save their life, and ours.

A real friend is a back seat driver *when justified*. This means reminding that friend that they are speeding, tailgating, driving in the blind spot of others, failing to use turn indicators when they turn, or recommending that they stop texting or talking on their cell phone while driving.

A real friend will also tell a friend that their car sucks, if it does. For instance, if the car brakes don't work or it has a tendency to catch on fire. And a friend who has a car that sucks wouldn't let a friend into their car if they *were a real friend*.

3

Friends tell their friends that they aren't acting like a friend, when they aren't.

A friend who: does things to hurt or upset you, tries to manipulate you, puts you down in front of others...see #100 for more, isn't being a friend.

A real friend will confront and discuss with a friend who isn't being a friend that they aren't. A friend who isn't being a friend needs to know that they aren't so that what they are doing does not destroy the friendship. (It might be that they forgot what it means to be a friend. If they did, they probably should read this book.) This is private stuff between you and your friend, so a real friend will discuss it *face to face* or put it *in writing*. Writing here *doesn't* mean in a text message or email or on a social media site. It means on a piece of paper or in a card. If they don't respond by changing what they are doing, it may be time to let them go – to ease out of the friendship.

4

Friends tell their friends when they are being a Dickhead.

Sometimes people just don't realize that they are being a Dickhead. A real friend will tell a friend who doesn't realize that they are being a Dickhead that in fact they are. It might be at a party when a friend has had too much to drink and is making a fool of themselves. Or maybe it's in a parking lot when a friend pulls into a handicap parking space when no one in the car is truly disabled.

No one likes a Dickhead and no one wants to be with a Dickhead, unless, of course, they too are a Dickhead. So that their friends aren't Dickheads, a real friend buys all of their friends the book, *Are You A Dickhead?* by Fred Mogura and *recommends* that their friends do the simple 100 question quiz in that book.

(Note: Being a Dickhead isn't just a guy thing. Girls too can be Dickheads.)

5

Friends tell their friends at Karaoke night that their singing is terrible, when it is.

A real friend will tell a friend when their singing skills aren't up to sharing with others, that they should stay away from the stage and the microphone at Karaoke night. This is most important if that friend also *tries* to dance while they sing.

Naturally, a real friend will tell that friend the facts – in private – *before* their friend gets up on stage. Giving a friend advanced warning that he or she sounds and looks like a real dork when on stage can save that friend the painful experience of having to listen to people, who aren't their friends, boo, hiss, complain and or laugh at them when and after they sing and or dance.

Of course, as a real friend, we don't and won't boo, hiss, complain or laugh at a friend if they fail to take our advice and do get up and sing.

6

Friends tell a friend when their butt crack is sticking out above their pants.

We see it all too often – a butt crack out there when and where it shouldn't be. Intentional or not, a real friend will tell a friend if and when that friend needs to tuck that baby back into their pants.

A real friend will also tell a friend if nose hairs are hanging out of their nose, funky hair is popping out of their ears or pubic hair is sticking out from places where it shouldn't be.

A real friend tells a female friend if they have a mustache that needs a bleach or shave, a unibrow that needs a good trim or mow, or if their panties need adjusting to fix that camel toe. A real friend will tell a male friend if mister happy needs adjustment so mister happy stops flopping around or is simply looking too happy.☺

7

Friends tell their friends when the clothes they're wearing or their latest hair style looks stupid.

A real friend will tell a friend if the clothes they are wearing look lame or make them look odd or stupid. It might be those red polka-dot pair of clown pants they love or the silk see-through blouse that they think is sexy that reveals lumpy things that really shouldn't be visible in public.

A real friend will also tell a friend if their hair style or the way they comb their hair must go. They won't hesitate to tell them that the *bee hive* hairdo looks stupid and needs to be dismantled or that the comb-overs aren't fooling anyone.

Same applies to those Mohawks, pointy hairdos and orange or multi color hair coloring. Noting that a real friend will do so *only if* it does look stupid, not simply because they don't like it.

8

Friends help friends to see the truth, even if the truth hurts.

A real friend will tell a friend how it *really* is, the truth, when the friend fails to see it themselves. By doing so, a real friend may help a friend to acknowledge issues or problems that need their attention. It may also help their friend to recognize solutions and create an opportunity to ask for *suggestions*. This can help improve or change things that aren't working in that friend's life.

It might be telling a friend that he or she looks tired or unwell and *they* recognizing the need to slow down, take a vacation or eat better. It may be that the friend has been doing strange things or often seems depressed and suggesting that the friend get professional help. It could be that the friend has a shitty job and suggesting that the friend learn something that would help the friend to get a better job. Or maybe a friend is a *real loser* and asking that friend why they are a loser and suggesting they get their act together.

PART 2

Communicate

One of the most beautiful qualities of true friendship is to understand and to be understood.

(Lucius Annaeus Seneca 5 BC – 65 AD)

PART 2

Communicate

9

Friends tell their friends when they are about to fart.

A real friend gives a friend as much warning as possible *before* they fart. Those who don't warn a friend or who let the friend know only as they are farting, aren't a real friend.

Warning a friend of an up coming fart can give a friend the opportunity to run to safer ground. In the event that evacuation is not possible, such as in an elevator, an early fart warning may enable a friend to prepare the best they can, under the circumstances. It might give them enough time to turn their head, hold their breath, cover their nose, cough or maybe join in with a fart.

No doubt, farting between friends can be a lot of fun. But there are times, places and situations when a fart is unwelcome. A real friend knows when to fart and when not to fart when with a friend. They know when to give warning, when and where to hold it, and when to let it rip.

10

Friends know how their friends are feeling without their friends needing to say a single word.

Real friends are able to read each others' actions and reactions, that is, their body language. For instance, if a friend is angry or sad, a real friend can see it in their friend's face or read it in their body posture, position or motions.

Body language is often unconscious behavior, and as such we often don't realize that our body is telling the real story, displaying our emotions and feelings. What our body tells our friends is hard, if not impossible, to hide from them.

A real friend takes the time and makes the effort to *watch*, *learn and recognize* a friend's body language. This enables a real friend to *see* what a friend is really thinking or feeling without that friend needing to say a word.

11

Friends share their true thoughts and feelings with each other.

Real friends truly *communicate* with each other. They share what they want to share and genuinely listen to what the other has shared. They also understand that sometimes a friend may not wish to share and want to be left alone to figure things out for themselves. In that event, a real friend is there if that friend later *decides* to share.

Real friends focus on understanding what their friend is sharing. They realize that doing so enables each other to better understand who the other is, what the other is thinking, how the other is feeling and what is important to each of them. They also realize that it enables them to work together to find answers and solutions where answers or solutions are needed. And they know that all of this leads to an even better, happier friendship.

18

12

Friends know what a friend likes.

A real friend knows what their friends like and dislike. They know because they have taken the time and made the effort to find out. They have watched, asked and listened. They don't simply assume that their friends like or dislike the same people or things, *simply* because they're friends. A real friend understands and appreciates that a friend may in fact not like or dislike the same people or things, and accepts that in a friend.

A real friend looks and listens for clues in what a friend is saying so to discover what that friend truly likes or dislikes. A real friend *reads between the lines* in what a friend is saying so to discover what their friend wishes or is trying to say when that friend is unable to say it themselves. For instance, maybe they are mad at something we did or that they like Dick or Jane when they really don't but say that they do so that other people will like them, but won't say so.

13

Friends have face-to-face interactions on a regular basis.

Today, so many people stay in touch with their *friends* via text messaging or email. No faces or body language. *Nothing to see* that may enable us to truly know what that "friend" might really be thinking or feeling. Little there to really learn about their friends – except possibly that they failed spelling or grammar in school.

Some people have *friends* they have never met, *meeting* on Facebook or some other social media platform. These *friends* could be using a photo of an animal, flower, clown or a sexy guy or girl as their profile photo. Who knows, they might in real life be a freak, weirdo or beast or someone's old wrinkled granny or grandpa.

Like with granny and grandpa, regularity is the key. A real friend will do whatever possible to have old fashion face-to-face interactions with their friends and as often as possible.

14

Friends truly listen to what a friend says.

Truly listening to what someone is saying means having the patience to hear what is really being said. It means paying attention. This means not butting in or commenting until *after* the person has finished saying what they want to say.

Real friends are good listeners. They *truly* listen. They don't interrupt when a friend is talking. They also don't argue a point or play the devil's advocate. They *genuinely* listen to their friend to find out what that friend is thinking or feeling.

They might disagree (friends do from time to time) with what a friend says, but a real friend lets a friend say what he or she wants to say. After it has been said, they might calmly nod or comment or present their point of view. If what's being said is turning into an argument, a real friend will tell a friend *before* it does and suggest that the topic be put on hold for another time.

15

Friends carefully read texts and emails from friends and reply or respond to them.

Friends send their friends texts and emails to share stuff, often to get that friend's response or reaction to what they have shared. Friends ask questions in texts and emails to get an answer, reaction or reply.

A real friend replies and responds to those texts and emails. Replying and responding lets their friend know that they did receive the message, and importantly, read the message. It also lets that friend know that they appreciate that friend sharing with them.

Replying and responding means replying with comments or thoughts on what was shared and answering questions asked. *Emojis* don't cut it. They are a lazy person's way of saying – I can't be bothered. Real words show that we do care.

16

Friends return a friend's phone call rather than wait for that friend to call them again.

Most people today often, if not always, use text or email messages to communicate with others. For many, using a telephone to communicate is uncomfortable, even avoided. A real friend will know if their friend is one of those who does and is. Knowing this, they'll know that a friend would have probably had a good reason to call.

Like with text and email messages, not getting back to (calling) a friend who called or taking a long time to do so is communicating to that friend that what that friend wants to share or has to say or wants to ask isn't important to us.

A real friend, even if they too are uncomfortable using or avoid the phone, *returns* a friend's call. Both win. One doesn't have to call again and the other hears what the other wants to say.

17

Friends ask friends "what's up" when something seems wrong.

A real friend *genuinely* cares about their friends. They want to know if something isn't right with a friend. If something doesn't seem right, they will ask a friend if things are OK. If their friend looks sad, stressed, worried, angry or a bit off – they will ask their friend why they look like they are. They will want to know and will ask why if a friend is acting odd or odder than usual. They will also ask a friend who seems to have less energy than they normally do or who has been doing things they normally don't do – why.

When a friend asks, a real friend will give that friend a truthful and intelligible answer. "I'm OK" from a friend who looks like **** isn't being *truthful*. Neither is a ☺ reply in response to an email asking how things are. What the **** does ☺ mean? But "I've been tired because I've been working a lot of overtime lately," or "Not good, my kid deleted my phone contacts today" are.

18

Friends truly communicate with their friends.

True communication among friends is all about sharing thoughts, ideas, feelings and opinions with each other. It's about friends being comfortable with saying what they want to say. It's about being comfortable asking and being asked questions and feeling comfortable giving honest answers to those questions.

A real friend, for instance:

- Tells a friend that what that friend is about to do may be something they shouldn't do, if they think it is.

- Tells a friend that the world is falling apart or that it needs more hot dog restaurants, if they feel like sharing that with them.

- Doesn't accept or say "I don't care" when they ask a friend or are asked by a friend *what they want to do*. Everyone does care.

PART 3

Support Each Other

The most I can do for my friend is simply be his friend.

(Henry David Thoreau 1817 – 1862)

19

Friends support their friends.

A real friend will do what they can do to help and support their friends so that their friends can be happy and can achieve their goals and dreams, whatever they might be.

To support a friend means being there for that friend. It means taking the time and making the effort to help or encourage a friend when that friend needs help or encouragement. It might be that a friend needs emotional, physical, mental, spiritual or possibly financial help or support.*

It may be as simple as going to a friend's golf or judo competition to cheer them on. It might be listening to a friend after a breakup. Or maybe it's traveling with them to a foreign country if the friend isn't ready to do it on their own.

* Noting that if a friend asks for or needs financial support, the giving friend does so cautiously and the receiving friend knows it's not free money and that it must be repaid to their friend as soon as possible.

20

Friends sticks around when things get tough.

A real friend is there no matter what's going on with their friend. They have their friend's back. They are there to support and watch out for a friend – stand up for, even physically defend, a friend, if need be.

A real friend sticks around not only during the good times but *also during* the not so good times. They don't bail on a friend if their friend is having a tough time or if their friend is faced with a difficult or serious issue. For instance, if once healthy now not so or once rich now poor, a real friend doesn't walk away. They are there to help their friend adjust or get through whatever it is.

Sticking around for a friend does not include times when things that a friend is doing or about to do could injury or kill us or get us thrown in jail. Anyone who would put our safety or freedom in jeopardy is not a friend.

21

Friends listen to what their friends have to say and offer suggestions or advice – only when asked for such.

A real friend knows when a friend *simply wants to talk*, wants a friend to truly listen to them – to act as a sounding board so that they can work out their problems or issues on their own. An "I see" or simple nods of the head may be all that a friend really wants or needs from a friend. A real friend doesn't assume that a friend wants or needs advice. They give advice *only if asked*.

A real friend will wait patiently for a friend to finish saying what that friend wishes to say. A real friend might ask questions so that they can *better understand* what the friend is saying. They may also do so knowing that the right questions might help their friend to better understand the problem or issue the friend is facing or dealing with (helping the friend to help themselves).

22

Friends know when it's time to stay, stop or go.

Helping a friend and being there for a friend is what real friends do. For instance, if at a friend's home and that friend is not feeling well, a real friend will want to help and therefore stay. But at the same time, a real friend will know when a friend wants to be alone, that it's time to stop and for them to go. For example, if a friend has the squirts and would really rather squirt alone, a real friend will say their farewells and go.

Even if a friend says it's OK, a real friend will know when "it's OK" really means it's not, that it's *time to stop and or go*. Say we're caught picking our nose and wiping it on a friend's sofa. A real friend knows "it's OK" means time to stop.

When it's time to stop and go, a real friend will politely excuse themselves and go. No hanging around hoping the friend will reconsider or beg them to stay. They will simply stop and go.

23

Friends wish only the best for their friends.

A friend's health, happiness and prosperity is a top priority for a real friend. They wish the best for their friends. They wish for their friends to have only good things happen to them.

A real friend is genuinely happy for a friend if a friend happens to be smarter, more successful or is better looking than they are. A real friend is also happy for a friend who happens to have a better job, makes more money or has a bigger, better or nicer house than they do.

Jealousy has no place in a true friendship. Nor does secretly sabotaging a friend's health, happiness or prosperity. A real friend would never wish that a friend falls on their face, lands on their back, loses a boy/girlfriend, goes bankrupt or dies. If you have "friends" who are jealous or who do wish these things, it's time for you to dump those "friends" and find new *real* friends.

24

Friends support their friends' goals, dreams and aspirations.

To be truly happy in life, we need to be healthy. We also need to be satisfied with what we are doing in our life. This means achieving *most* of our goals, living *most* of our dreams and having and doing *most* of what we desire in life.

Real friends want their friends to be *truly happy* in life. To help them be so, they ask their friends what *they truly desire* in life and encourage them to get it. They do what they can do to help their friends to actualize their goals, dreams and aspirations. It might simply be asking a friend about their goals and dreams. Maybe it's giving them a pep-talk or well-deserved *pat on the back* as they get closer to reaching them. Or maybe it's providing physical or financial help to do so.

People who would do otherwise, that is, those who are jealous of, criticize or try to sabotage our goals, dreams or aspirations, aren't friends.

25

Friends are positive when with friends – even if things appear or are grim.

When things are tough, look worse than they may be or seem to be or are out of control, we need to believe and feel that we will get through it all. We need to be and remain positive. A real friend can provide us with the support we need during those times in order to be and do so.

Things might not seem so hopeless when with a friend who is positive. By being positive, a real friend can help a friend to remain positive and in control, reassuring that friend that things will be alright.

Knowing that we have someone who's *genuinely* concerned about us and is there to support us gives us hope. *Hope* is what enables us to overcome or deal with the tough, negative or grim things, events or problems that we face in life.

26

Friends help their friends without having to be asked.

If a friend is troubled or in trouble and needs help, a real friend will recognize it. A real friend *knows* when a friend needs help. They can sense it. They don't need their friend to ask for help.

When a friend seems to be in need of help or obviously needs help, a real friend will do what they can do to help their friend. When it's time to help, a real friend knows the difference between helping and preaching, lecturing or telling a friend what to do or how to do it.

If a friend is being or is about to be verbally or physically attacked, a real friend will *step in* and do what they can to stop or deflect the attack. If a friend is doing or is about to do something that is dangerous, wrong or illegal, a real friend will *remind* that friend that what they are doing or are about to do may not be the right thing to do. If need be, they will stop it from happening.

27

Friends do what they can so that their friends are happy today and in the future.

To help a friend be happy, a real friend knows what their friend truly likes and enjoys doing – what makes them truly happy. No assumptions. For instance, if we like small dogs or eating hot dogs, that doesn't mean that our friends necessarily like the same.

A real friend also knows when a friend is a bit off or isn't happy, without needing to be told so. A real friend simply know when a friend's mental, emotional or physical well-being is suffering.

When a friend isn't happy, a real friend will ask their friend *what's wrong*, why the friend is suffering. A real friend will not accept a "Nothing's wrong" from the friend. They will do what they need to do to find out what's going on so that they can help their friend to get and be happy.

28

Friends scratch their friend's back.

This may apply literally, that is, to lend a friend a hand to scratch an itch that they are unable to reach themselves. But it can also mean that a friend is willing, and in most cases happy, to help a friend when that friend needs help with something that they can't do themselves.

Often it's doing something that helps a friend get what he or she needs or wants but is difficult or even morally or socially unacceptable for them to do it themselves. For instance, it might be asking a friend to put in a good word (*stretch the truth*) about them with someone they want to take out before they ask that person out.

A real friend will scratch a friend's back without the expectation of them scratching theirs later on in return. And if a friend is a real friend, they won't ask a friend to do it often or to do something that is not morally or socially acceptable.

29

Friends help friends find solutions to their problems.

A real friend is there and ready to help a friend with a problem. It might be a problem a friend recognizes on their own. Or it might be something a friend sees in a friend that the friend doesn't see themselves. Either way, a real friend doesn't attack a friend with nasty comments but rather *attacks the problem* (helps find a solution).

A real friend is only interested in helping their friend work out their problem. For instance:

- If a friend is really overweight, a real friend doesn't call that friend gigantor or chunky. A real friend would organize time with that friend to exercise together, to lose weight.

- If a friend loses their job, a real friend won't call the friend a loser. A real friend *will work with* their friend to determine exactly why they lost their job and help the friend determine what they can do to get another job.

30

Friends help friends to mend or overcome a difficult past.

Many of us have made decisions in life we now wish we hadn't made. Some of us have said and done things in life that we wish we hadn't said or done. Some of the decisions made and acts done may have *resulted in* a difficult or bad past, a past that is having or will have a challenging or negative effect on one's present or future.

A real friend might not agree with the decisions and acts a friend made in their past. But if they are a friend, a real friend will do what they can to help that friend to overcome or deal with the consequences of any wrong or bad decisions or acts that friend made or did.

Maybe it's to help a friend get through rehab. It might be to help a friend to mend a broken self-esteem after a bad marriage or to rebuild their confidence having failed in school. Or it may be to help a friend to re-invent themselves.

PART 4

The Right Thing

We secure our friends not by accepting favors but by doing them.

(Thucydides 460 BC – 395 BC)

31

Friends offer their friends a drink and or a snack soon after coming to their home.

Rather than wait for a friend to ask for a drink when at their home, a real friend asks the friend if they would like something to drink. They will also ask their friend if they would like a snack – chips, candy or maybe a hot dog or burger.

What you offer isn't important, pretty much any-thing will do. What is important is that it must be in or on a clean cup or plate, something fresh and offered fairly soon after the friend arrives. The cola or glass of wine on the kitchen counter from last night or last night's left over meatloaf or spam still on the dining table – won't do.

A real friend wants their friends to feel and be comfortable when at their home. One of the best ways to do that is with a drink to quench their thirst and a bite to eat to quell their hungry.

32

Friends buy a book that a friend wrote or a music CD that a friend recorded.

Writing a book or recording original music are both something to be proud of. It takes a lot of time and effort and often comes from the heart. It's something that's truly important to the person who wrote the book or recorded the music.

A real friend is truly happy for a friend who has written a book or recorded music. They appreciate their friend's achievement. They're excited to read the book or listen to the music, even if the book isn't their area of interest or the music isn't their type of music. A real friend knows it's the right thing to do. (It might be really good).

A real friend will tell their other friends about the book or CD. They'll mention it on Facebook or their blog. They might also write a review on the website where they bought the book or CD.

33

Friends go to performances that a friend is performing in, directing or producing.

Performing in, writing, directing or producing a play or show is something that's very important to the person *who* performs in, writes, directs or produces it. Attending the play or show may be the best way to show a friend that what they do in their life is important to us, that we care.

A real friend acknowledges that what a friend does with their time is a part of who they are. Taking an interest in what our friends do with their time gives us an opportunity to learn more about a friend. The *more we know* about a friend the closer and stronger a friendship can become – exactly what a real friend hopes for.

Who knows, we may discover that we enjoy or would like to do the same thing, which we *may not have discovered* if we hadn't taken an interest.

34

Friends help friends to change or improve things that their friends feel bad about themselves.

Feeling good about ourselves requires having a healthy level of self-esteem and self-confidence (a lot but not too much). Our self-esteem and self-confidence directly affect our emotional and mental health. Both play a major role in determining whether we are happy with who we are and whether we can do what we want to do in life with people we want to spend our life with.

A real friend helps a friend to realize this. Then they work with that friend to help their friend to take steps to improve their self-esteem and self-confidence. It might be to go to the gym with them to get fit so that they can feel better about their body (self-esteem). Or maybe it's to encourage them to go back to school to learn more so to realize they can do more (self-confidence).

35

Friends are willing to change their plans to help out a friend.

Problems, tough times and times when things just aren't right sometimes occur when we may be unable to handle those things on our own. A friend can often make it easier for us to overcome or deal with those problems and times.

It may be when a friend's car breaks down and that friend needs a ride to work. It could be a friend who needs to go out of town who needs a friend to take care of their granny or someone to feed their cat while they are away. Or it might be a friend who simply needs a friend to talk to.

Rarely are plans so important that they can't be changed. A real friend will do what they can to change or adjust their plans if doing so would help a friend. This doesn't mean allowing someone who claims to be a friend to take advantage of that willingness to do so. Nor does it mean to allow someone (friend or not) to do it too often.

36

Friends apologize when they are wrong, made a mistake or failed as a friend.

For some people it's hard to say "I'm sorry." For some it's even harder to admit that they were wrong, made a mistake or that they did something that a friend would not do.

Love means never having to say you're sorry is only for the movies – not real life. A real friend will admit when they're wrong or has made a mistake. They will think about what they did or did not do to learn from it so that they won't do it again. They will promptly and sincerely apologize if an apology is due. A real friend knows that a prompt and sincere apology can help to mend and make a friendship stronger.

A simple sincere sorry goes a long way. People who can't admit to being wrong or can't say that they are sorry, aren't and can't be a real friend.

37

Friends use proper manners when in public with friends.

When with friends, most of us will at times goof around, maybe even make a fool of ourselves. But there's a line that should never be crossed.

A friend might be a Dickhead, but a real friend never acts like a Dickhead when in public with friends. For instance, they would never *unload* a loud juicy fart at a friend's wedding as the bride is walking down the aisle. Though it may get a few laughs from other Dickheads at the wedding, it could lead to more than merely upsetting or annoying those sitting near the farter.

A real friend always has a friend's feelings and best interest in mind. This means knowing and following proper etiquette when with friends in public. Lack of manners and etiquette can easily embarrass a friend. It can leave a long-lasting bad feeling. It could even put a friend's health and safety, even life, at risk.

38

Friends pay back money they borrowed from a friend as soon as possible.

When cash is in short supply, it sure makes life easier to have a friend who is willing to lend us some. It might be a few dollars to buy enough gasoline for the car to get home. It may be a few hundred or so to get the car fixed and back on the road. Or maybe it's a few thousand to buy a new (used) car.

A friend who loans money to a friend shouldn't need to remind or ask that friend to pay them back. Even if the friend who lends the money is super rich, a real friend will pay them back and will do so as quickly as they can. This doesn't mean first buying a new smart phone when the one you have now is working fine. Nor does it mean going to Vegas before you do. It means making paying them off your first priority, being thrifty, a tightwad, until they have *been paid back*.

39

Friends tell the truth tactfully.

A real friend aims to always be truthful with their friends. At the same time, they are always sensitive of their friends' feelings. So, sometimes an indirect truth (being tactful) is better than insensitive hurtful facts.

A real friend knows how to tell the truth tactfully, to get the truth told in a sensitive manner, to help a friend to realize the truth *without* hurting their feelings. For instance, if a friend's breath smells like dog poop, a tactful way to tell that friend might be to say something like, "I have noticed that you've lost your toothbrush. Here's a few bucks to buy new one." A wink may help.

Tact is *how something is* said, how it's delivered. Think about it. Would you rather a friend tell you that you really stink, or for them to tell you that you can use their shower until you can get your shower fixed? They should get the hint.

40

Friends take the blame for their own actions.

Real friends take *full* responsibility for their own actions and reactions. A real friend would not blame a friend for the consequences of the actions or reactions they took. If they made a mistake, had done something wrong or something didn't go as planned, they take responsibility (the blame). For instance, failing an exam. A real friend wouldn't blame a friend who insisted on going out the night before the exam*. They could have said "No." (*A real friend wouldn't ask.)

Blaming a friend for something that the friend didn't do can suck the friendship out of a friend. It can lead to serious emotional issues within a friendship and can result in distrust in and resentment towards a friend.

Joking, like blaming a friend for a fart, is acceptable between real friends. But blaming for pretty much anything else might not be. Be careful.

41

Friends call before they go over to a friend's home.

We all enjoy the freedom to wear what we want to wear (or to not wear anything at all) when in the privacy of our own home. We also all enjoy the freedom to do things we want to do without others seeing us doing them. A *surprise visit* from anyone can put us in an embarrassing or awkward situation. Or we might simply be too busy doing things to have a friend in our home.

A real friend respects their friends' privacy. This means that a real friend doesn't suddenly show up at a friend's front door. They will call *before* going over to get the AOK from their friend that it's OK to stop by.

At the same time, a real friend can sense when a friend doesn't really want them to go over, even if that friend says it's OK to come over. A real friend *listens between the lines* and when the time doesn't seem right, will suggest another time.

42

Friends go to their friends' graduation, and even to their friends' kids' graduation too.

Graduating from school and university is a big deal and means a lot to those who are graduating. It also means a lot to the families of those who are graduating, be it kindergarten, elementary, middle or high school or university.

A real friend knows this and if invited will take the time to attend a graduation ceremony and or party of a friend or friend's family member. Like weddings, graduations are an *I am happy to be here to celebrate this event with you* time. It's a great opportunity to show our friends that we *genuinely* care and are happy for them and their family members' accomplishments.

A friend is sure to appreciate their friends being there far more than any texts, emails, cards or gifts they might receive from their friends. Unless not invited, not being there when you can be there is telling a friend that you don't care.

PART 5

Walk the Walk

Actions, not words, are the true criterion of the attachment of friends.

(George Washington 1732 – 1799)

43

Friends thank friends with words followed by action.

Real friends show their friends that they appreciate what those friends have said or done. They
say *thanks* or *thank you* in person, or via phone if
they genuinely can't do so in person. A *thanks*
or *thank you* in a text, email or on Facebook may
do, but doing so in a text, email or on Facebook
can lack that genuine feel of appreciation.

They also follow those words with action, they
do something a little extra. It may be buying or
making a tangible *Thank You* card and sending
it to the friend via snail mail. It might be paying
for that friend's latte the next time they go out
for a coffee together. Or maybe it's buying that
friend a fun or small gift or doing a *similar* thing
in return for the friend, if the opportunity arises.

It's not the *what is done* that's important. It's the
doing that is. A real friend will take the time and
make the effort to do that little extra.

44

Friends send via snail mail or give their friends in person a *real* birthday card.

When was the last time you sent a friend a real birthday card – bought or made a card, put a postage stamp on it and *mailed* it or handed it to a friend? Think of the last time you received a real card. Remember how happy it made you feel? Probably as happy as your friend did feel.

Real friends show their friends that they care by taking the time and making the effort to do a little more than what's normally done in this computer/electronic gadget society we live in. This includes remembering a friend's birthday by snail mailing or delivering in person to that friend a real birthday card. (Even better – see 45)

Got to ask yourself – if a friend doesn't have the time or can't be bothered to snail mail or to give you in person a simple birthday card, are they really a friend?

45

Friends take a friend out for a coffee or meal on a friend's birthday or when a friend seems a little down.

Birthdays are important, even if the person who is having a birthday says they aren't. It doesn't need to be celebrated with a party or a chocolate cake. A coffee or meal with a friend is likely to make the person having a birthday feel liked or loved. That's a *great* celebration, gift and feeling.

Same applies when things aren't right, when a friend is feeling a little down. A coffee or meal with a friend is likely to make that friend feel a little better knowing that someone cares.

A real friend will of course pay for that coffee or meal. They will never ask to split the bill or put their hand out expecting their friend to fork out their share of the bill. A real friend will refuse all offers from their friend to pay for their share – with an "it's my treat" and a smile.

46

Friends make their friends smile.☺

It doesn't take much to make a friend smile. A happy story or event or remembering fun times together can bring on a smile. A warm or nice (honest) comment or a small gift for no reason at all can also make a friend smile.

A smile touches the heart of both the one who smiles and the person who see that smile. What better way to say "I enjoy being with you" than to smile with a friend.

A smile can make a friend's day a little nicer. It can take a friend away from their worries and troubles, even if for only a few minutes. A smile can bring friends closer together, may even lead to something positively unexpected, even frisky.

A friend might tell a joke, do a little dance, sing a song or flex their butt checks to get their friend to smile. Doesn't matter what, as long as it does.

47

Friends laugh with their friends, not at them.

Laughing with friends is one of great things in life. But laughing at a friend is probably one of the worst things someone can do to a friend.

Real friends know how far they can joke with a friend. That is, a real friend knows what might offend or hurt a friend's feelings. They understand a friend's sense of humor and know the topics, issues and things that a friend is sensitive about. They also have a pretty good idea of how a friend feels *about themselves*, for instance, if they are self conscious of their body.

A real friend knows that knowing all this stuff helps them to avoid crossing the line when with their friends. It greatly minimizes the chances of offending, hurting or laughing at a friend. They will also stay watchful of a friend's reactions, as such may be a signal that a line is about to be crossed, and will pull back so that they don't.

48

Friends truly appreciate their friends.

A real friend is there to listen to our grips, ideas and feelings. They support us when support is needed and help us deal with and get through tough times. They listen to our jokes and laugh with us. They are truly interested in us and are there to help us to grow and to become who we really wish to be. Having *real friends* adds to our happiness and satisfaction in life. They can even help us to live a longer and healthier life.

Real friends truly appreciate all the many things their real friends do and contribute to their life. They treasure their friendship and recognize the true value of that friendship.

A real friend lets their friends know how they feel about them and their friendship. They do so by being a real friend, saying things like thank you, sorry, how can I help..., doing things without expecting things in return, and truly caring.

49

Friends try to reason with a friend when doing so is in that friend's best interest.

Although real friends let their friends be themselves, to make their own choices and decisions and to do what a friend thinks is right, a real friend will step in when they feel their friend is about to do something they (*as a friend*) believe isn't best for that friend.

A real friend will take the time and make the effort to try to *talk sense into* a friend who is talking about doing or is about to do something stupid, rude, nasty, dangerous or illegal.

At the same time, a real friend will know when reason (talk) isn't enough, that they need to step in and take some sort of action. For instance, a real friend would *physically restrain* a friend from starting an argument or fight or getting into one that he or she is certain to lose, swimming in the ocean when drunk or punching a police officer.

50

Friends aim for time spent together to be positive and fun for both themselves and their friends.

No one *in their right mind* wants to have a rotten time when with their friends. They don't want to return home after time with a friend saying to themselves – "Boy, I had a really crappy time".

A real friend wants to enjoy time spent with a friend and for that friend to also enjoy the time. This means *being positive,* not spending the time talking about or doing negative things or going to negative places. A positive time is a fun time.

If getting together with a friend is to talk about problems, negative things or simply to *complain*, a real friend will tell their friend *in advance* that's the reason for getting together. A real friend will also see to it that something *positive* comes from it, for instance, a positive solution to a problem.

51

Friends "like" or comment on a friend's Facebook posts.

Most people have a Facebook account to share stuff with their friends. Some share their photos. Some share stories about their kids. Some may complain about their boss or their job. Others post YouTube videos about issues that are important to them or that they think are amusing.

Of course they also want to see and read about things that are happening in their friends' lives: things on their friends' minds and what's going on in their lives. But let's face it – *the main reason* most people have Facebook is to get their stuff out there, to share with their friends.

Like in real life, if "friends" don't react to what we share, it can feel like our friends don't seem to care. A real friend reacts. A real friend *likes* or comments on their friends' posts. A simple click of the *like button* or a comment such as "it made me laugh" to most posts should do the trick.

52

Friends want to make their friends laugh so hard that they pee or poop their pants.

Real friends are fun to be with. They are fun to be with mainly because they *get us*, they know who we are and what makes us laugh. We can be ourselves, be goofy and let it all out.

Laughing with friends is great for our health and for our relationships. A good laugh helps us to release our inner self. It's good for our face and ab muscles. It can also lead to many great memories and an even closer bond.

Having a sense of humor is key. So too is being with a friend who does get us. Other than that, *pretty much anything* can be funny. For instance, a nice *friendly fart* with a friend can get things rolling, make them laugh – sometimes so hard they too fart, even pee or poop *their pants*. When was the last time you made a friend *really laugh*?

53

Friends are patient with friends when need be.

Friends can sometimes be trying or annoying. Sometimes they may complain about the littlest things. Sometimes they talk about stupid things. Other times what they talk about are things we would rather not talk about. And sometimes we may wish that they would just shut up.

Friends can sometimes do things that we think are stupid. Sometimes what they do or the way they do things *annoys* us. Other times what they want to do are things we would rather not do. And sometimes we may just feel like punching them in the head for those things.

A real friend doesn't make rude faces or nasty comments, nor do they tell a friend to shut up. A real friend doesn't punch a friend in the head. A real friend remains *patient*. They find the earliest *opportunity to change* the topic of discussion or the activity, or excuse themselves and leave.

54

Friends let a friend win sometimes even if they aren't as skillful.

Everyone hates to lose, especially if every time at everything they do. Losing all the time is like being kicked in the head, a painful reminder of what a *loser* they are. No one wants to be a loser.

Have you ever played racket ball or tennis with a friend who beats you every single time? You probably smile when they say "good game" as you leave the court after you lost the game, yet again. Maybe you're saying to yourself, "What a Dick". Or maybe inside you are hoping that they slip in the shower or that a big black dog bites them on the way home.

A real friend will let a friend win from time to time. They congratulate them and will never tell *anyone* later on that they let them win. But when they do let them win, they ensure that it looks like a real win – that it wasn't an *I let you* win.

55

Friends clean up after themselves when they are at a friend's home.

We shouldn't need to *clean up* after friends. This includes friends who: vomit or allow food to fall out of their mouth onto our floor, leave poop marks in our toilet bowl, pee on our toilet seat, or leave hair or gunk in our bathroom sink.

A real friend is *conscious* enough to know if they have made a mess. If they have, they clean up after themselves without needing to be asked to do so. And they don't wait for or accept "Don't worry about it, I'll clean it up" from a friend.

This doesn't mean that a friend needs to do our floors, clean our bathroom or wash the dishes (it would be nice though). Nor does it mean that a friend should strip the bed and wash the sheets after *fun in bed* (unless it was fun-in-bed-alone fun). It means a real friend cleans up any mess they make straight away or before they leave.

56

Friends are good passengers when in a friend's car.

Have you ever had someone in your car who treated your car like a city bus? Have you ever had someone barf in your car?

A real friend *knows how* to be a good passenger. They know that throwing trash on the floor of a friend's car is not the thing to do. They know they shouldn't pick a booger and stick it underneath the seat or in the glove-box when riding in a friend's car. They also know that this also applies to digging out ear wax or scrapping off other body substances and rubbing it on their friend's car seat. And *of course*, they know never to throw up in a friend's car.

A real friend would stick their head out the car window to barf, stick the booger in their pocket or eat it when no one is looking, rub any body substance on their own clothes and take their trash with them when they get out of the car.

57

Friends check that their shoes are clean before entering a friend's house or getting into a friend's car.

No one wants sticky crewed gum or wet smelly dog poop on their carpet or in their car. Nor do they want mud or any other unidentifiable substances stuck on their carpet or in their car.

A real friend will:

- Look at the bottom of both their shoes *before* entering a friend's house or getting into a friend's car to ensure that they are both free of gum, poop or *anything* that a person with half a brain wouldn't want on their carpet or in their car. Or

- Always have clean socks on and take their shoes off *before* going into a friend's house or getting into a friend's car.

58

Friends act responsibly when out with friends.

Most of us probably don't have a problem with Dickheads or idiots – as long as they aren't with us or trying to *interact with us*. In fact, *watching* a Dickhead or an idiot or someone who is dealing with a Dickhead or an idiot can be entertaining.

A real friend knows that irresponsible behavior when with friends can embarrass their friends. They also know that it *can ruin* the time for their friends and *may even destroy* the friendship.

When out with friends, a real friend doesn't do Dickhead things or act like an idiot. This means they don't cause trouble, complain or fart too much. They aren't noisy and aren't a nuisance. They also never drink so much that they end up barfing up everything they ate and drank, have trouble standing up or pass out. If they drink, *they* keep their eye on how much they drink, so that their friends don't need to do it for them.

PART 6

Respect Each Other

Criticize your friends privately, but praise them openly.

(Publilius Syrus 85 BC – 43 BC)

59

Friends give their friends total freedom to be themselves.

Real friends appreciate and accept us just the way we are. They don't try to "improve" or "fix" us so that we meet their standards or agree with their rules, opinions or philosophy. A real friend doesn't preach or try to impose upon us their beliefs and values or moral code. They never try to pressure us to be who we aren't or do things that we don't want to or would rather not do. They respect us and let us be who we are.

But at the same time, real friends do care about their friends and want them to *better themselves*, to become more of who they really want to be.

When a friend recognizes in a friend potential for betterment and growth, a real friend will let that friend know what they see and believe. If the friend asks for suggestions or advice, a real friend will share their *thoughts and ideas* on what and how the friend might better themselves.

60

Friends know what would hurt a friend's feelings.

A real friend would never deliberately do or say anything that may hurt a friend's feelings. They are always careful with *what they do or say* when with a friend so that their friend doesn't feel offended or take it as an insult or personal attack.

This requires knowing what upsets, bothers or embarrasses a friend. It means *knowing who* that friend *really* is, their beliefs, values and sensitivities – so not to do and say things in a way that might offend or hurt that friend. It also means taking care in what we say to others when talking to others about our other friends.

It doesn't mean not doing or saying what we wish to do or say. It means knowing how to do and say things when with that friend. It means doing and saying the things we want to do and say *tactfully*, in a manner sensitive of a friend's personality, beliefs, values and insecurities.

61

Friends care less if their friends are ugly, fat, skinny or a complete idiot.

True friends take their friends for who they are, inside and out. This includes their looks, body shape and size, and intellect or lack of. A real friend would never make their friends feel that they should or need to hide any of their physical features or traits from them.

A real friend is happy to be with their friends. They overlook the occasional stupid things their friends may do or say when in public. They like their friends even if those friends aren't at their best, for instance, if a friend looks a bit dumpy, is having a bad hair day or argues with staff at Starbucks about a 5 cent overcharge.

Being a real friend means looking at the inside rather than the outside of a friend. It means not being a *Shallow Hal*. (If you don't know what that means, watch the movie by the same name.☺)

62

Friends care about *who* not *what* a friend is.

Maybe you're a student, school teacher, office worker, a builder of some sort, an IT person, a doctor, lawyer or an artist or maybe just a bum. Maybe you're rich or famous or maybe you're broke. It might be that you're a mom, dad, wife or husband. Or maybe you're something else.

A real friend is fine with whatever a friend may be. It's not important to them *what* a friend is, as long as that friend is OK with what they are. A real friend wants their friends to be *who* they are and likes them for *who* that is.

A real friend is a friend because they like us for *who* we are on the inside. It's our personality, attitude, standards, beliefs and values, social and moral philosophy, likes and dislikes and things that we care about. For a real friend, social and job titles, fame or money are not *who* a friend is but rather *what* a friend has achieved in life.

63

Friends want to know what their friends think and believe.

Our thoughts and beliefs are the foundation of *our attitude*. Our attitude directly motivates our behavior. It determines *who* we are, *what* we do, *how* we handle things that happen to us in life and *how* we associate with others.

A real friend wants to understand *what's behind* the what, how and why their friends do and say what they do. One way to do that is to discover what a friend thinks and believes by asking that friend what they think and believe. When a real friend does, they don't criticize or attack a friend for their thoughts or beliefs, they *genuinely* listen to and consider that friend's answers because they truly want to know their friends.

If too many of those thoughts and beliefs are not the same or similar, a real friend might decide that maybe they shouldn't be a friend at all.

64

Friends keep themselves out of their friends' private affairs, unless invited.

For any friendship to remain healthy, all those in the friendship must respect each other's privacy – keep their nose where it belongs.

In a healthy friendship, there's *my business*, *your business* and *our business*. There is also *my life*, *your life* and *our life*. A real friend recognizes the difference and sees the value in keeping things that way.

Minding *my* and *our* business and life proves to our friends that we *respect their privacy*, that their past and personal matters that don't relate to us are theirs unless they wish to share it with us. For instance, a real friend will not ask a friend about past lovers (their business) unless that friend is sharing. Nor would they show up at a friend's private event (their life) unless invited.

65

Friends respect their friends to make their own choices and decisions.

The choices and decisions we make in our life can make all the difference in our life. They play a major role in who we become. They can get us closer to or drive us further away from where we wish to be. They can even destroy our life.

A real friend doesn't apply peer or social pressure to try to influence a friend's choices or decisions. This means that a real friend never pressures a friend into doing something the friend may feel isn't right for them. For instance, a real friend wouldn't try to convince a friend to get drunk or stoned or to be like everyone else.

A real friend does, however, apply *positive* pressure. In other words, *they encourage* their friends to choose or decide to do something that their friends want to do or know would be beneficial to them if they do but need a little push to do.

66

Friends trust their friends.

Trust in a friend means having a strong belief in the truthfulness and reliability of that friend. It means not having to worry that a friend will lie to them, reveal their secrets or walk away.

Trust in a friend means believing that the friend will be supportive of and will look out for them. It means being *confident* that the friend will help them out when they need a helping hand. For instance, a friend would feel safe knowing that a friend would help them stay on track if things got tough when making changes in their life.

Real friends share a mutual trust in one another. This makes for a *rewarding* friendship. It enables friends to be open to share their most private thoughts and deepest feelings. This helps them to work out their problems or worries they may have. It also enables them to feel safe and more confident. This in turn encourages them to do things and try things they haven't done before.

67

Friends only say good things about a friend to others.

Chances are when you were a kid someone told you – "if you don't have something nice to say about someone, don't say anything at all". This applies as much, if not even more, now as it did when we were kids. In fact, the consequences of *not following this advice* are very likely to be more severe and longer lasting today than they were when we were kids.

Gossiping or saying something nasty about, or putting a friend down behind their back is not being a friend. Doing so can hurt, even destroy, a friendship if what was said about that friend ever gets back to that friend, which chances are it will. Trying to defend what was said is likely to fail and hurt feelings may never be mended.

Real friends respect their friends and will *defend* a friend (who is or isn't there) against those who do speak badly about their friend.

68

Friends know and respect their friends' values.

Values are behavioral and emotional ideals; principles, standards or preferences concerning *appropriate* actions, reactions or outcomes. They're concepts that we believe are important in life (our life in particular) about what and how we and other people *should* think, feel and behave.

Our values define our personality and character. They influence our attitude, beliefs, choices and decisions. They play a major role in what we do and how we do things. They determine how we treat others and how we wish and expect others to treat us.

A real friend knows what their friends value. They respect their friends' values by supporting their friends to *freely express and live* their life by *those values*. Like with thoughts and beliefs, if too many aren't the same or similar, a real friend may decide that they shouldn't be a friend at all.

69

Friends respect their friends' way of doing things.

We all prefer to do things our own way – to live our life the way *we wish* to live it. Maybe we like to go to sleep really early or very late. Or it may be we prefer to spend our time in quiet places or like places filled with activity and noise.

A real friend respects how their friends wish to live their life. It might be that they wish to:

- go out to a non-smoking or quiet restaurant, or a restaurant filled with smoke and noise – when out to dinner with friends.

- be called or sent text messages at anytime or not before 8 or 9 am or after 9 or 10 pm.

- stay home or go out with close friends, or to go out wherever with whomever, even with people they don't know.

- be left alone, or to be pampered when they have the poops or are down with the flu.

70

Friends respect the privacy and dignity of their friends.

We all should be able to decide what we share with others – to keep our stuff and information private *if we choose*. It may be something we did, something about us or, what most of us likely consider to be most private, our naked body.

We all share a common value and worth, that is, we are human beings. As such, we all should be seen, heard, listened to and treated fairly – to be valued and respected and not mistreated or neglected. (Dignity)

A real friend respects and protects their friends' privacy and dignity. They know that intrusion into or revealing personal or private information about a friend or failure to respect a friend's dignity can embarrass, humiliate, even diminish or destroy a friend's *self-worth*. And they know this can have a negative effect on how a friend feels about themselves, and thus their *happiness*.

PART 7

Consider One Another

Friends cherish one another's hopes. They are kind to one another's dreams.

(Henry David Thoreau 1817 – 1862)

71

Friends keep their promises unless genuinely unavoidable.

A promise is an assurance, a commitment that one will or will not do something. It might be a friend promising us that they will help us build a shed in our garden on Saturday. Or it might be they promise us that they won't forget to call us. Whatever it may be, we often plan what we will do based on what others promise they will do.

Let's say, for instance, someone tells us that they will pick us up at the airport. We make *our plans* based on that. That is, rather than take a taxi or train from the airport, we look for them at the airport and wait for them if they're running late.

A real friend honors their promises. If unable to keep a promise, they let us know *as soon as* they know that they can't keep their promise. If running late, they apologize and let us know when they'll be there. Or if they cannot do what they promised, they ask if they can do it another time.

72

Friends who have sex together wish it to be fun for all of those in bed together.

Sex is meant to be fun – real fun. A real friend knows this. They *know* that *fun sex* is not simply an in-and-out affair. They know that it requires communication between friends in bed so that all those involved are happy and satisfied with the input and outcome.

A real friend also knows that the timing needs to be right and that sometimes the time is not right. They know it's not something to rush into nor is it something to rush to finish.

A real friend will ask a friend in bed what they like. They will *truly listen* to what the friend says he or she enjoys and wants in bed. This enables all those in bed to put the right thing in the right places at the right time so that everyone in bed can have fun.

73

Friends thank each other for the things they do, including the small things.

Saying *thank you* is so easy to do but so many people seem to have trouble saying it. A simple "thanks" from a friend shows us that our friend *values* our friendship and truly appreciates what we have said or done.

Gratitude, even a simple *thanks*, often makes us happier and even healthier. It motivates us to do more of the same in the future. This in turn is likely to strengthen a friendship even further.

For a real friend, anything kind, major or minor, large or small that a friend says to or does for us is something to be thankful for. For instance, if a friend tells us they like our unusual haircut (and mean it), we're *quick* to thank them. If they buy us a ten cent piece of candy that we don't particularly like, we thank them the same.

74

Friends turn off their cell phone, tablet or computer when out for lunch or dinner with friends.

When with a friend, a real friend will give their friend their utmost attention. They choose to be with the friend because they wish to truly interact with them. This means that they don't use or stare at their phone, tablet or computer when with them. A real friend chooses to *turn off* these devices and puts them away – out of sight.

If expecting an important call or message, a real friend will tell their friend that they are expecting such. A real friend will, however, after saying so, keep the device *off* the table (on their lap) and will concentrate on being with their friend.

Who could honestly say that they enjoy being with someone who is playing with or constantly looking at a phone, tablet or computer. *Can you*?

75

Friends are considerate of their friends' time.

A real friend is considerate of and careful with a friend's time. They accept that their friends might not always want to do the things they like or want to do, or with whom they want to do it with. They understand that a friend may have other plans or that they would rather do something other than something else. For instance, it may be their friend would rather stay at home than to go out and party with Jack and Jill.

A real friend will ask their friend if they want to join them in doing something *before* things are organized. In other words, a real friend doesn't make plans that include their friend without first asking their friend if he or she does or doesn't want to be a part of that plan. If that friend does not want to or can't be, a real friend accepts that. A real friend doesn't apply pressure nor do they get angry with their friend. In fact, a real friend is happy that their friend is honest with them.

76

Friends reply to text messages and emails from a friend.

Doesn't it annoy you when you send a text or email to a friend and that friend doesn't reply? Doesn't it annoy you if you ask a question in a text or email and the friend you sent the text or email to doesn't answer your question?

For most of us, *we send* texts or emails to friends to *communicate*, share or ask a question. No reply or response from that friend is simply telling us that they don't care. A simple "Fine" to *How are you?* or "Yes" or "No" to a question may be all it takes. Same applies to no comment on a photo. A simple "Nice photo" may be all that's needed.

A real friend *replies or responds* to text messages and emails as soon as possible or practical. This includes answering questions or giving a reason for not answering questions, and commenting on any attached photos – in a text message or email. Never too much trouble for a real friend.

77

Friends desire a value for value relationship.

Value for value means *to give something to receive something of similar or same value of that which was given*. Value for value in a friendship means that *each person* in the friendship feels that what they give to the friendship is of similar or same value (to them) as that which they receive.

A friendship is a *give-and-take* relationship. That is, each person needs to give something in order to get something they need from the friendship. For instance, one person may want someone to talk to and the other wants someone to spend time with. If a friendship isn't a give-and-take relationship, it's likely that the friendship will falter or fall apart sooner rather than later.

A real friend aims to give as much (preferably more) as what they take (receive). A real friend doesn't keep score, but they *won't accept* always giving more than they receive, for too long.

78

Friends call or send a text or email after a night out to ensure that their friend(s) has returned home safely.

A real friend wants to know that their friend(s) get home safely after a night out together. They will take a minute (might take even less) to call or send a text message or email to their friend(s) to ask if the friend(s) has arrived home safely. They will do so soon after they think that their friend would have arrived home.

A real friend will promptly replies to that call, text message or email. It doesn't require much. Something as simple as, "I'm home, thanks", "Thanks, it was great" or simply "Good night" should do. How hard can that be?

If out with others who aren't as skilled as you at defending yourself, a real friend will take those friends to their door to ensure they do get home.

79

Friends ask how a friend is feeling and are genuinely concern about their response.

If you're not feeling well and a friend asks you how you're feeling, how would it make you feel if after you told them, for instance, you've been barfing, their response was – "That's nice"?

"That's nice" when things aren't right might be OK for a stranger or someone we dislike, but it's definitely not OK for someone we call a friend.

A real friend truly cares about a friend's well-being. When a friend looks troubled or looks as if they aren't at their best, a real friend doesn't ignore it. Nor do they start talking about their troubles or how they feel. A real friend will ask a friend how they're feeling. They will *genuinely* listen to their friend's answer and be *genuinely* concerned with their friend's reply. They will then ask their friend what they can do to help the friend to feel better/be right.

80

Friends always have time or will make the time to see, talk to or spend time with a friend.

Being a real friend means a lot of things. Three of those things are to: see (face to face), talk to (in person) and spend time (real time in person) with a friend.

We have all surely at one time or another told a friend that we have been *so busy* that we haven't had the time to see, talk to or spend time with them. In other words, we didn't have the time to be a friend.

A real friend will always have the time or will do whatever they need to do to make the time to see, talk to and spend time with their friends. Anyone whose life is so busy that they don't have or can't make the time to do so, needs to change their *priorities*, find a different career or job or make changes to their lifestyle.

81

Friends call or visit a friend who is a bit down.

Hearing a friendly voice or seeing an ugly, not so ugly or good looking face of a friend is sure to help anyone who is down to feel even just a tad bit happier. A real friend knows this. They will make the call to or visit that friend, even if just to talk or visit for a few minutes.

At the same time, a real friend will recognize and understand if the friend desires to be left alone. In other words, a real friend will realize when a friend doesn't want to talk or be visited. This requires *listening between the lines* of what a friend says. For instance, "You can come over *if you want*" may mean please don't come over.

When a friend is a bit (or a lot) down, it isn't the time to talk about our problems over the phone or to invite ourselves over to eat their food, drink their beverages or to watch *Naked Alone* on their 70 inch television. It's time to think about them.

82

Friends who smoke are considerate of their friends who don't.

Some of us are fine with smoke filled rooms or smoke that mysteriously always seems to float right into our face, regardless of where we are standing or sitting. But some of us aren't.

A real friend who does smoke *won't smoke* when with friends if it might *bother* friends who don't. This applies in their home and a friend's home. It applies in their car and a friend's car. It can also apply when in public with a friend. If they wish to smoke, a real friend will simply do so away from friends, or even outside so that the smoke doesn't end up on and in a friend.

A real friend who doesn't smoke, even though *concerned about* the health of a friend who does smoke, doesn't nag or put their friend down for smoking. But they will from time to time *remind* that friend that they do care about their health.

PART 8

Be A True Friend

There is nothing on this earth more to be prized than true friendship.

(Thomas Aquinas 1225 – 1274)

83

Friends help friends recognize when they're doing things they shouldn't or may not realize they're doing.

Sometimes we might not recognize that we are being a Dickhead or an idiot or simply being inconsiderate. For instance, it might be:

- picking our nose and flicking what we pick.
- speeding or tailgating when driving.
- stopping in the middle of a busy sidewalk to answer and talk on our phone.
- standing in front of an elevator door when doing so blocks those who want to get off from getting off when the doors open.

A real friend wants us to be *who we are*, but they will let us know if and when we're doing things we probably shouldn't. They know that doing so can help us to be a better person.

84

Friends feel happy for a friend if that friend knows more, can do more or has done more than they have.

A real friend is not jealous of their friends. They are happy for their friends and may *admire* them for what they know, can do or have done. If it's something they would like to know or do, they will ask that friend if they will share with them how they too can gain the knowledge or ability needed in order to know or do the same. (Which a real friend will share.)

A real friend knows there is a difference between *jealousy* and *admiration*. They know jealousy can be negative and unhealthy, and can often lead to resentment. They also know that admiration is often positive and healthy – as it can be a constructive desire for something that, if positive action is taken, can help to make them and their life better and happier.

85

Friends let their friends lead and to be on top from time to time.

Some of us can't seem to get the opportunity to lead or to take control. For instance, it might be that we always miss out on being chosen to be the team leader of a project at school or work so that we can lead. Or it may be that we are never able to get on top so that we can take control, for instance, when in bed with a friend.

A real friend will give a friend the opportunity to lead and to be on top. Doing so enables that friend to learn and to get better at leading and taking control. In fact, in some situations, letting a friend lead or take control can make it easier, less work, more relaxing, lead to a better outcome or even more fun for us (the person being led or controlled). How can we know what our friends are capable of doing if they don't have the opportunity to do it from time to time.

86

Friends expect nothing in return except friendship.

A real friend doesn't look for or expect fringe benefits for being a friend, other than *friendship*. They simply like a friend for *who* that person is, not for the benefits that person may provide.

Let's look at two scenarios.

- My name is Suzy. I'm a hottie. I drive fast and fancy cars, go to expensive restaurants, exotic destinations and private clubs, and hang out with the rich and famous. I'm a nasty bitch. I'd scratch your eyes out if it would get me something I want.

- My name is Dick. Not the best looking guy. I drive a 1975 Ford, eat at home, vacation in my backyard, am a fork club member and hang out with my cats and a homeless guy. I'm kind and honest. I've got your back.

Who would you want to be your friend? Really?

87

Friends can be who they really are when with a friend.

Have you ever had a friend who was truly odd looking, smelled bad, never seemed to comb or wash their hair, farted a lot, often picked their nose, wore old dorky clothes, would sometimes walk around for days with a giant zit on their face or food in their beard (if they had one), and or who seemed like they weren't all there? If so, congratulations! You were truly a *real friend* to that individual. If you haven't, you're lucky!

Chances are, however, a person who *would* take on the *above individual* is probably also truly odd looking, smells bad, doesn't comb or wash their hair, farts a lot, picks their nose, wears dorky clothes, walks around with zits on their face or food in their beard (if they have one), and or is likely missing more than a few of their marbles.

The point is – if we can't be who we really are when with someone, they aren't a *real friend*.

88

Friends are loyal and trustworthy.

A real friend knows what it means to be loyal. They know that being loyal means being truthful and expressing how they truly feel – being straightforward with a friend. They know that it means being *supportive* of a friend – willing and prepared to support and defend that friend. A real friend also knows that it means not being a manipulator or taking advantage of a friend.

A real friend knows what it means to be trustworthy. They know that it means consistently being dependable, following through on their commitments and promises. And although they know that a real friend supports their friends, they know that being trustworthy means that a friend can rely on them to *not* support them if they're wrong or are planning to do something that might not be right or good for them. And if so, they will tell them so and set them straight – with their friend's best interest in mind.

89

Friends look out for and after each other.

Imagine a friend (Jill) standing by watching you getting drunk at a party. Now imagine that you are really drunk and are getting into a car. You see Jill laughing as she waves at you as you drive away in the car. Jill is more interested in laughing at you than looking out for you.

Imagine a friend (Jack) taking you aside at the party *before* you get drunk and saying to you that he's concerned and thinks you should stop drinking before you are really drunk. Imagine you not listening to Jack and Jack wrestling you to the ground to stop you from getting into that car. Jack doesn't preach to you. He simply tries to talk some sense into you before you do something that may really screw up your life.

Although not a baby sitter or a preacher, a real friend *will look out for and look after* their friends. Jack or Jill? Who would it be for you?

90

Friends can be trusted to be a reliable confidant.

A confidant is someone who is told things that are private, secret or sensitive and is trusted to keep those things private or secret. A confidant can be a friend we choose to share and discuss our private, secret and personal stuff with, who we trust will not share it with others.

Having someone who we can talk to about our most private thoughts and feeling and personal stuff (knowing they won't share what we talk about with others) can help us to relieve stress. It can provide us with a safe environment that may enable us to dig deeper into ourselves, as we are likely to feel more comfortable sharing with that friend. This may help us to help ourselves to discover and to fix, improve or change things that aren't right in our life. It also enables us to explore and discuss dreams and goals. All of this may help us to get more in and from life and lead to a healthier and happier life.

91

Friends aim to have a positive impact on their friends' lives.

A real friend wishes their friends happiness and satisfaction in life. They also want to contribute to and have a positive impact on their friends' lives. To do so, they aim to help their friends to become who their friends truly wish to be doing what their friends really want to do in their life.

A real friend will do what they can to encourage, support and help a friend to achieve their dreams, goals and aspirations. It might be that they help to boost a friend's self-esteem or self-confidence, if boosting is needed. Maybe they *brainstorm* with a friend to help the friend better understand what they need to do to get what they want. Or it might be that they help a friend to identify their skills and talents and help that friend to find or create a way to utilize them to achieve their dreams, goals and aspirations.

92

Friends help their friends feel good about themselves.

A real friend will recognize when a friend is in need of a little help to feel better about who they are. When they do, they'll do what they can do. When feeling down, a friend can help a friend to feel better. If a friend is feeling a little dumpy, lumpy or dumb, a friend can help that friend do something about that feeling – help them so that they don't feel dumpy, lumpy or dumb.

A real friend might help a friend to feel better about themselves by giving that friend a few positive words of encouragement. They might take that friend shopping to help them to pick out some clothes that wouldn't make them look so dumpy, or take them to the gym so that they aren't so lumpy. They may even try to convince that friend to read more books or to take a class at the local college so that the friend doesn't feel dumb or so down on themselves.

93

Friends share.

Most of us shared things with our friends when we were a kid. Maybe it was a secret. Maybe we shared our gummy bears. Or maybe we shared our bike with them when riding to school (we had a bike, they didn't) or our lunch at school (a bully often took their lunch money). Whatever it was, we shared. That's what friends did.

Now that we are adults, sharing plays a more important role. In addition to the bond sharing creates between friends, things we can share as an adult could help a friend live a happier and healthier life. It could even save their life. For instance, sharing credit with a friend at work for a job well done may help the friend to get a promotion at work. Or sharing a fact learned from a visit to the doctor *may* extend or save their life.

We can share almost anything with a friend. But somethings should probably never be shared, like underwear, lipstick, a toothbrush or lover.

94

Friends are happy to do things from time to time the way a friend does things.

Some people like to plan things before they do things, others like to do things spontaneously. Some people like to send and get texts anytime of the day or night, others don't send or answer texts between 11pm and 7am. Some people like to eat dinner at 6, others like to eat it at 8. Some make their bed in the morning and others just before going to bed.

It's very unlikely that our friends do everything the same way we do things. And it's very likely that the way a friend does some things *may even* bug the crap out of us. A real friend, although not giving up the way they do things, will from time to time *without complaining* do some things the way a friend does things when they are with that friend. (This is assuming that it isn't illegal or dangerous, such as texting while driving).

95

Friends wish to spend quality time with their friends.

We see it everyday everywhere, people who are with people they call a "friend" who are playing with electronic *devices*, such as a tablet or phone; playing video games, texting, fixated on a social media website or looking at stuff online. Others are day-dreaming, staring into space or pulling stuff out of their nose or ears and examining what they pulled out. What's up with that?

Real friends want to and do spend *quality time* when with their friends. They know that quality time is all about uninterrupted time, truly being there time – in full mind, body and spirit. They know it means looking at that friend and truly communicating with the friend *face-to-face*. They also know that it means doing stuff *together* that means something. It might be talking about local or world events, taking a road trip or overseas trip or working out at the gym. Together stuff.

96

Friends are focused on the friends they are with.

Real friends are truly tuned in and focused on the friend(s) they are spending time with. They give their full attention to the conversations they are having with that friend(s). This means that they are *genuinely listening* to their friend(s) and don't and won't allow anything but a major distraction to interfere with doing so.

Take for instance, Jack and Jill are having a coffee at Starbucks. Someone Jack knows walks up to their table. Jack suddenly stops the conversation he's having with Jill. He turns to and talks with the person who came to the table for 10 to 15 minutes. If Jack were a real friend, he would have first said to Jill something like, "Sorry Jill, excuse me for a minute" *before* he started to talk with that new person. And Jack would only talk with that person for a minute or two, at most, then would focus back on Jill. Same applies to text messages, emails and phone calls.

97

Friends show their friends that they care about them.

There's no better way to show a friend how we feel about them, *regardless* of sex or sexual preference, than a pat on the shoulder, a light touch in the appropriate place or a genuine hug.

Most women touch and hug friends, male and female, to *show* their friendship or concern. Men *can* and should do the same. Touching and hugging doesn't need to be sexual or make one feel uncomfortable. All one needs to do is to let go of the misconception that a touch or a hug is or should be sexual, that it should lead to sex.

A real friend knows that they need to follow a few simple rules to keep touches and hugs from being sexual. 1. Keep their hands off of and their *stuff* away from contact with their friend's *stuff*. 2. No humping, pumping or body rubbing, and 3. A slight touch or small squeeze is all it takes to let a friend know that they do *care about them*.

98

Friends forgive friends even if they don't forget.

In a friendship, we all make mistakes and do things (big and small) that we shouldn't have or wished we hadn't done. A real friend *knows* this and in most cases accepts that what happens in a friendship is a consequence of being a friend. They are able to forgive a friend for *pretty much* anything that a friend says or does.

A real friend would probably forgive (but might not forget) a friend borrowing their car without asking. A real friend may forgive (but is likely to never forget) a friend who accidentally ran over their cat or dog.

But there are some things that a friend (even a real friend) wouldn't and shouldn't forgive or forget. These include: taking advantage of or stealing from a friend, stabbing a friend in the back, punching a friend, and trying to mount or successfully mounting a friend's partner.

99

Friends pay their own way.

Maybe you have a bighearted friend – a friend who always pays for things, like coffee, lunch or beers, when you go out with them. Maybe they always drive their car when you out together so you don't have to use the gas in your car. Or maybe when out shopping and you *casually* say to that friend that you like that red sweater, you find that while you were busy taking a dump, they bought you (paid for) that same sweater.

Having a friend who can do all this is great. But allowing a generous friend to always pay is not being a real friend. A real friend makes a sincere effort to pay their own way (their share), at least more times than not.

A real friend doesn't accept the first *It's OK. I'll pay*. They pay. If the offer comes a second time and they decide to let their friend pay, a real friend will thank their friend and will do something nice for them soon after they pay. (See 43)

100

25 Things Friends Should *NEVER* Do:

1. Talk about a friend behind their back.

2. Pressure a friend into doing something that friend doesn't want to do.

3. Bring up or talk about things (history) that bothers, hurts or embarrasses a friend.

4. Apply double standards in the friendship.

5. Brag or only talk about themselves.

6. Under-estimate a friend's intellect or ability.

7. Vandalize, steal or lie when with a friend.

8. Keep their phone in their hand all the time when they are out with their friends.

9. Put their phone next to the bed when in bed with a friend who's trying to have fun.

10. Eat the last of anything in a friend's fridge.

11. Tell a friend that the friend really screwed up – that the friend is an idiot for doing or saying what they did or said.

12. Flirt with a friend's lover, partner, mother or father.

13. Invite themselves to come over or stay over at a friend's house.

14. Put their hand down their pants and move their hand around when on a friend's sofa.

15. Call or text a friend after 10pm – *unless* it is an emergency or that friend is expecting or had previously said that it's OK after 10pm. The same applies to unexpectedly showing up at a friend's front door after 10pm.

16. Take a video of a friend when naked, doing things naked or doing stupid things and post it online or save it to use at a later time, such as if their *now friend* later isn't a friend.

17. Call a friend a Dickhead when that friend is in fact not a Dickhead.

18. Waste a friend's time by constantly showing up late, continually canceling appointments or not showing up at all.

19. Fail to turn on the water facet when using a friend's bathroom if they are farting while taking a poop – knowing that their friend in an other room can hear them farting.

20. Use a pair of a friend's panties, underwear or a sock in that friend's laundry basket to clean up poop marks left in a friend's toilet.

21. Post photos or private information about a friend on social media without *first* asking that friend if they are OK with such being posted. This includes group photos.

22. Give out a friend's phone number, address or other personal details *without* first asking that friend if it's OK with them to do so.

23. Tell a friend that they know how that friend is feeling when in fact they don't.

24. Borrow money from a friend and forget that they did or if they didn't forget, change the subject when that loan is brought up.

25. Pretend to be a friend so that they can look cool, ride in a fancy car, get free stuff, free lunch, free booze, entry into a private club, even to get into someone's pants.

Epilogue

We all want to believe that we are someone's friend and that they are ours. We may think that we are a good friend, but in fact we may not be. We may think that those we call a friend are our friend, but in fact they might not be.

It's impossible to be a real friend – if we don't know what it *means and takes* to be a real friend. But, if we do know, it's not that difficult.

Is it worth the time and effort? Most definitely. No doubt it takes extra time and effort to be a *real friend*, but being one can make all the difference in our life. When we are a real friend to others and have real friends in our life, we experience a richer, happier, more fulfilling and, some claim, longer life.

It's our choice to be a real friend to someone. It simply requires knowing what it really means and takes to be a real friend and then doing and acting as a real friend does.

It's also our choice who we choose to be our friends. We can choose people who we will call a "friend" or choose people who will be a *real* friend. Once we know how to be a real friend, we simply need to find people who do and act as we know a real friend does.

We all need to *stop*, *observe* and *think about* what we do and what those who we call our friends do so that we can determine if, in fact, we are genuinely someone's friend and they ours.

This book has given the reader the opportunity to review what it means and takes to be a *real friend*. It's now up to the reader to be one and to choose those who will be his or her real friends.

Mahatma Gandhi said, "Be the friend you want to have." Are you? Do you treat your friends the way you would like them to treat you? Do they treat you the way you want to be treated?

Always remember:

The only way to have a [real] friend is to be one.
(Ralph Waldo Emerson 1803 – 1882)

I wish you a rich, happy and long life being a real friend with real friends. Thanks for reading.
Fred Mogura

If you enjoyed this book, your review on Amazon or your favorite online book seller's website, Facebook or other social media site or blog would certainly be most appreciated.

Other Books from Simple Logic Publications

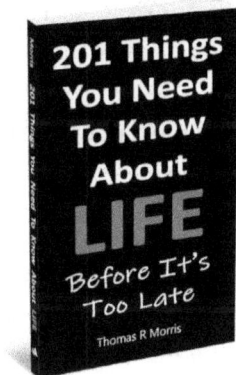

201 Things You Need To Know About LIFE Before It's Too Late
Thomas R Morris

This book is perfect for anyone who wants a head start in life. It's also for those who want to get their life back on track. It's filled with "I wish I knew this before I graduated high school or college" stuff.

Creating and living the life of your dreams is a Do-It-Yourself project. You need the right information. Then you need to do what you need to do with that information to make it happen.

This book looks at 201 things that may help you to do just that. The 201 things (+ 40 bonus things) in this book aren't difficult. They simply need to be read, understood and acted on. They may enable you to do more, see more, love more, experience more, get more of what you want in life a lot quicker, and make your life a lot happier and easier.

Here are a few of the 201 things in this book ↓

If you want to get things done better, *forget* about *multitasking*. Multitasking may lead to more being done but….

We start to die from the day we are born. Most of us look at life as years ahead of us rather than years we have *remaining*. Don't….

An average life is fine for those who can't do better. We can do better if we choose to do better. Don't accept life's default, merely….

Life isn't fair or unfair, it's just life. Feeling that life is unfair or that you got a raw deal isn't going to make things better. It will, however….

In the end, it's not the years in your life that count. It's the life in your years. Chances are when we reach the end of our life, we will….

Minimum wage sucks. If you don't have a plan in place that will enable you to earn a good income, ….

You don't need to have sex to be cool. Most people in school who talk about having a lot of sex are….

Are You A Dickhead?

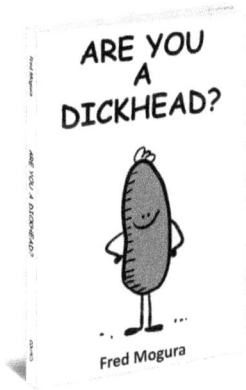

Ever wonder if *you might be a Dickhead*? Maybe you aren't really sure what makes someone a Dickhead. Or it could be that you aren't a Dickhead but you know someone who is, someone who does not know that they are in fact a Dickhead, and you want them to know that they are.

If so, this book is for you.

Are You A Dickhead? asks the reader 100 simple questions and provides simple multiple choice answers. By answering these questions, the reader is able to generate a score. This score enables the reader to determine:

- If they are in fact a Dickhead
- Whether they are a borderline Dickhead, or
- They are OK, they aren't a Dickhead.

From inside *Are You A Dickhead?* ↓

When in public, do you: (Question 1)

R   Pick your nose and look at what you picked.

U   Pick your nose and flick whatever you picked out into the air.

A   Pick your nose only when you know for sure that no one is looking or watching.

D   Pick your nose and eat what you have picked out.

H   Pick your nose and put what you picked out into your pocket to eat later.

When riding on a plane, train, bus or subway, do you: (Question 34)

R   Stink (have BO) or reek of garlic.

U   Allow your body to lean onto someone you don't know who is seated next to you.

A   Fall asleep on the shoulder of someone you don't know who is sitting next to you.

D   Sit with your mouth wide open, snore or drool, or all of the above.

H   Smell kind of nice, allow the person sitting next to you to have and use their space by keeping your body parts in your part of your seat, and always ensure that your mouth doesn't hang open and that you don't snore or drool.

www.ingramcontent.com/pod-product-compliance
Lightning Source LLC
Chambersburg PA
CBHW072158020426
42334CB00018B/2063

9780987267788